I'm a little teapot

I'm a little teapot, short and stout.
This is my handle and here is my spout.
When I get all steamed up, then I shout,
'Tip me over and pour me out!'

Let's begin

Say the rhyme. Pretend to be teapots and mime the actions.

Collect

Different teapots.

Count the number of teapots each day.
Sort them into order of size.

Teapot design

Say the rhyme.
Look at the teapot display.

What do you think makes a good teapot?
Think up some ideas.

Look at one pot. Ask questions about it.

* Why is it this shape?
* What is it made out of?
* Who does it belong to?
* How can you hold it?
* When can it be used?
* Where can you put the pot when it is hot?

Make a large classroom picture of a teapot and point out all the parts which make up a teapot.

Activity 3

Sorting teapots

Say the rhyme.
Sort the teapots into sets.
Try good pourers/bad pourers.

✳ Test your pots for pouring.
✳ Which ones dribbled?
✳ Why did some dribble?

Sort the pots into other sets by testing them.
Here are some examples.

pots which are easy to hold

pots which are hard to hold

pots which are heavy

pots which are light

Designing and making a teapot

You will need
plasticine

Let's design and make a pretend teapot out of plasticine.
Are real teapots made out of plasticine? If not, why not?

Ask yourself questions about the making of the teapot.

✳ What will the teapot look like?
✳ How big will the handle need to be?
✳ Which kind of spout will the pot have?
✳ Who is the teapot for?
✳ Does the teapot need to be large or small?

Activity 5

Testing the teapots

Make a class display of the plasticine teapots.

Tell your class about the teapot you have made.

✳ Why did you make it that shape?

✳ Who is going to use it?

✳ Is it easy to knock the teapot over?
Why do we have to make it hard to knock the teapot over?
Think about safety.

✳ Is it easy to hold?

Play with your teapots.

Which teapot holds the most?

Choose 3 teapots from the class display. You need to find out which holds the most water.

Can you think of ways to test this?

Perhaps you could count the number of cupfuls you need to fill the teapots.

Make a chart for the 3 teapots to show the results.

Remember to fill the teapot and cups up to the very top.

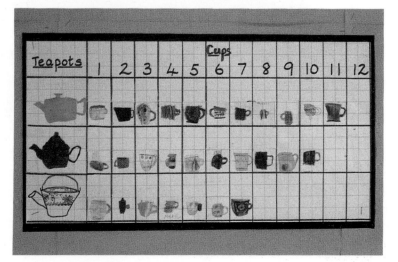

Inventors and inventions

Why did someone invent the teapot?
Pretend that teapots haven't been invented. What could we use instead for a teapot?

Ideas! Ideas! Ideas!

Collect

Things which we could use for teapots.

Start an inventors' table for new ideas for teapots.

Materials

Inventors need to know about materials. Look at the inventors' table.

✳ How many different materials can you see?
✳ Which materials could you use for the teapot?
✳ Which materials could you not use?

Think up different tests for the materials.

Try wetting some objects.

What happens?

Try bending some objects.

What happens?

What other tests can you think of for testing materials for teapots?

Activity 9

Drinks

What do you drink at breakfast time?

Make a class chart to record all the drinks you like at breakfast time.

You will need

felt-tip pens

address labels

paper

Write your name on labels. Take it in turns to stick the labels onto the chart.

Count up the numbers in each row. Which is the most popular drink?

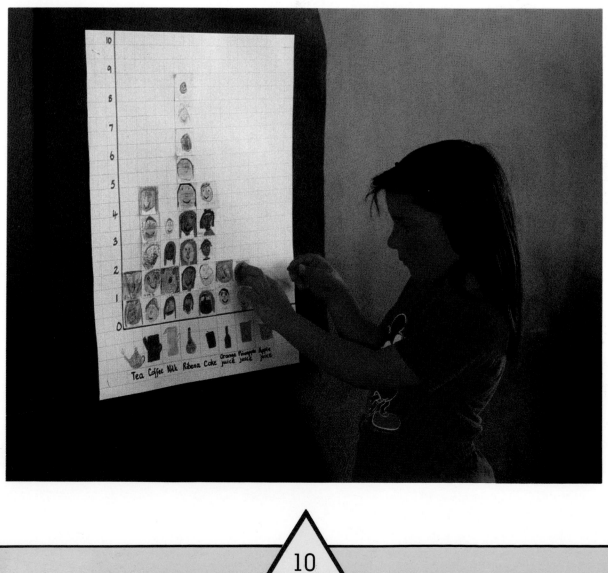

Finding out about tea

Where does tea come from?

Collect

Different types of tea.

Look at the different teas you have collected from home.

Think about how teas

look   feel   smell

Sort them into different sets.
For example:
    small leavesl/large leaves   dark leaves/light leaves

Where does tea come from? Do we grow it in this country?

Here is a picture of a worker in Sri Lanka picking tea leaves.

Activity 11

A guessing game

Talk about the different types of tea you have found.

Make some mystery smell pots.

You will need

elastic bands

tea

yoghurt cartons

tissues

Fill the pots with different types of tea which don't smell the same.

In small groups, try and guess which tea is which.

Let's make tea!

Do you know how to make tea?

Let your teacher make a pot of tea. Before your teacher makes it, ask questions about how to make it.

✳ What should we do first? Why?
✳ What should we do second?
✳ What should we do third?
✳ When do we switch on?
✳ How do we make sure everything is safe?
✳ Who do we have with us at home when we make tea?

Let your teacher try out two of your ideas.
Time them with a sand timer.

Which was quickest? Can you improve on it?

Make a class flow chart of the quickest way.

Activity 13

Making tea hot

Some people like their tea hot.
How long do you think the tea would stay warm in the pot?
In some pots the tea goes cold very quickly. Look at your teapots, which do you think would cool quickly?

Test whether each pot is the same. Choose 3 pots. Put some warm water in the pots from the same jug.
Put the same amount of water in each pot to keep everything the same.

✳ How long do you think you should leave the pots before you feel them?

✳ Do you find any differences between the pots?

How could we help the teapots keep the tea hot?

Ideas! Ideas! Ideas!

Making a tea cosy

A tea cosy is an invention.

Collect

tea cosies

Which tea cosies do you like best?

Invent your own tea cosy.

You will need

your ideas for materials   staples   tape

Ask yourself questions about it before you start.

✳ What do I need?   ✳ What shape do I make it?

✳ What can I use?   ✳ Should it be large or small?

Choose the two best ideas for a tea cosy and make them.

Ask yourself questions about it before you start.

✳ What material would be best to make it in?

✳ What shape do I make it?

✳ Should it be large or small?

✳ How do I join materials together?

Try stapling

Try sticking

Try out some ideas. Decorate your tea cosy.

Activity 15

Testing your tea cosy

You will need

teapots  sand timer

Test out your tea cosy on two teapots which are the same. Fill them with warm water.

Try one pot with the cosy and one pot without the cosy.
Leave for five minutes. Time using the sand timers.
Feel the pots and the water.

* Do they feel warm or cold?
* Do they feel the same or are they different?
* Does the tea cosy make a difference?
* Why does it make a difference?

Show your cosy to your friends. Look at their cosies.

Make a display of tea cosies.